This book belongs

Additional prayers by Meryl Doney and Jan Payne
Illustrated by Veronica Vasylenko

This is a Parragon book
This edition published in 2006

Parragon
Queen Street House
4 Queen Street
Bath, BA1 1HE, UK

Manufactured in China
ISBN 1-40544-410-X

# My Little Book of Prayers

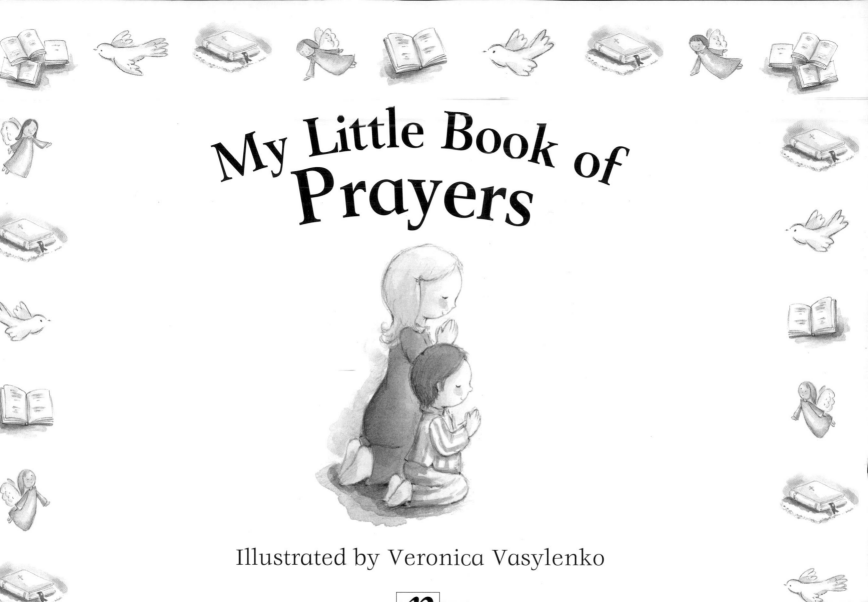

Illustrated by Veronica Vasylenko

*p*

For this new morning and its light,
For rest and shelter of the night,
For health and food, for love and friends,
For every gift your goodness sends,
We thank You, gracious Lord.

*Anonymous*

Our Father in heaven,
Hallowed be Your name.
Your kingdom come,
Your will be done,
On earth as it is in heaven.
Give us today our daily bread,
And forgive us our sins,
As we forgive those who sin against us.
And lead us away from temptation
And deliver us from evil,
For Yours is the kingdom,
And the power, and the glory,
Forever and ever.

Amen

1. Wide as the world,
   (spread arms wide)

2. Deep as the sea,
   (point down deep)

3. High as the sky,
   (point up high)

4. Is your love for me.
   (hug yourself)

Peace be to this house
And to all who dwell here.
Peace be to those that enter
And to those that depart.

*Anonymous*

Saviour, teach me, day by day,
Love's sweet lesson to obey;
Sweeter lesson cannot be
Loving him who first loved me.

*Jane E. Leeson (1807-82)*

Lord, teach me all that I should know;
In grace and wisdom I may grow;
The more I learn to do Thy will,
The better may I love Thee still.

*Isaac Watts (1674-1748)*

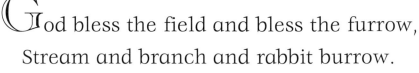

G od bless the field and bless the furrow,
Stream and branch and rabbit burrow.
Bless the minnow, bless the whale,
Bless the rainbow and the hail,
Bless the nest and bless the leaf,
Bless the righteous and the thief,
Bless the wing and bless the fin,
Bless the air I travel in,
Bless the mill and bless the mouse,
Bless the miller's bricken house,
Bless the earth and bless the sea,
God bless you and God bless me.

*Anonymous*

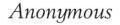

God bless all those that I love.

God bless all those that love me.

God bless all those that love those that I love,

And all those that love those that love me.

*From an old New England sampler*

Little deeds of kindness,
Little words of love,
Help to make earth happy,
Like the heaven above.

*Julia Carney*
*(1823-1908)*

Thank you, God, for giving us
The hippo and rhinoceros.
For crazy monkeys, brash and loud,
Giraffes with heads stuck in the cloud.
Thanks for parrots bold and bright,
And zebras smart in black and white.
For elephants with giant feet,
And anteaters so trim and neat.
I wouldn't want the world to be
Empty except for you and me.

To all the humble beasts there be,
To all the birds on land and sea,
Great Spirit, sweet protection give
That free and happy they may live!

Dear Father, hear and bless
Thy beasts and singing birds,
And guard with tenderness
Small things that have no words.

*Anonymous*

God bless the animals
Great and small,
And help us learn
To love them all.

Jesus, may I walk
your way
(point to your feet)

In all I do
(hold out your hands)

And all I say.
(touch your fingers
to your lips)

Amen

Thank you for flowers,
Thank you for trees,
Thank you for grasses
That toss in the breeze.
Thank you for vegetables,
Thank you for spice,
Thank you for everything
That makes food taste nice.
Thank you, dear Father,
For all things that grow
In sunshine and rain,
And the glowing rainbow.

HAPPY BIRTHE

Bless us, O Lord, and these Thy gifts
Which of Thy bounty we are about to receive.
Through Christ our Lord.
Amen

Be present at our table, Lord;
Be here and everywhere adored.
His mercies bless and grant that we
May strengthened for Thy service be.

*Traditional*

For what we are about to receive,
May the Lord make us truly thankful.
Amen

*Anonymous*

Here are the apples,
Here are the pears,
Crusty bread
And cream éclairs;
Potatoes and onions,
Barley and rye,
Honey in pots
And rhubarb pie;
Berries and cherries
And bales of hay;
Thanks be for the harvest
God gave us today.

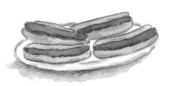

Father, we thank Thee for this food,
For health and strength and all things good.
May others all these blessings share,
And hearts be grateful everywhere.

*Traditional*

Now the daylight goes away,
Saviour, listen while I pray,
Asking Thee to watch and keep
And to send me quiet sleep.

Jesus, Saviour, wash away
All that has been wrong today:
Help me every day to be
Good and gentle, more like Thee.

*Rev. W.H. Havergale (c.1877)*

Day is done,
Gone the sun
From the lake,
From the hills,
From the sky.
Safely rest,
All is well!
God is nigh.

*Anonymous*

Day by day, dear Lord, of Thee
Three things I pray:
To see Thee more clearly,
To love Thee more dearly,
To follow Thee more nearly,
Day by day.

*St Richard of Chichester (1197-1253)*

Matthew, Mark, Luke and John,

Bless the bed that I lie on.

Four corners to my bed,

Four angels round my head,

One to watch and one to pray

And two to keep all harm away.

*Traditional*

I see the moon,
And the moon sees me;
God bless the moon,
And God bless me.

*Anonymous*

Now I lay me down to sleep,
I pray Thee, Lord, Thy child to keep:
Thy love guard me through the night
And wake me with the morning light.

*Traditional*

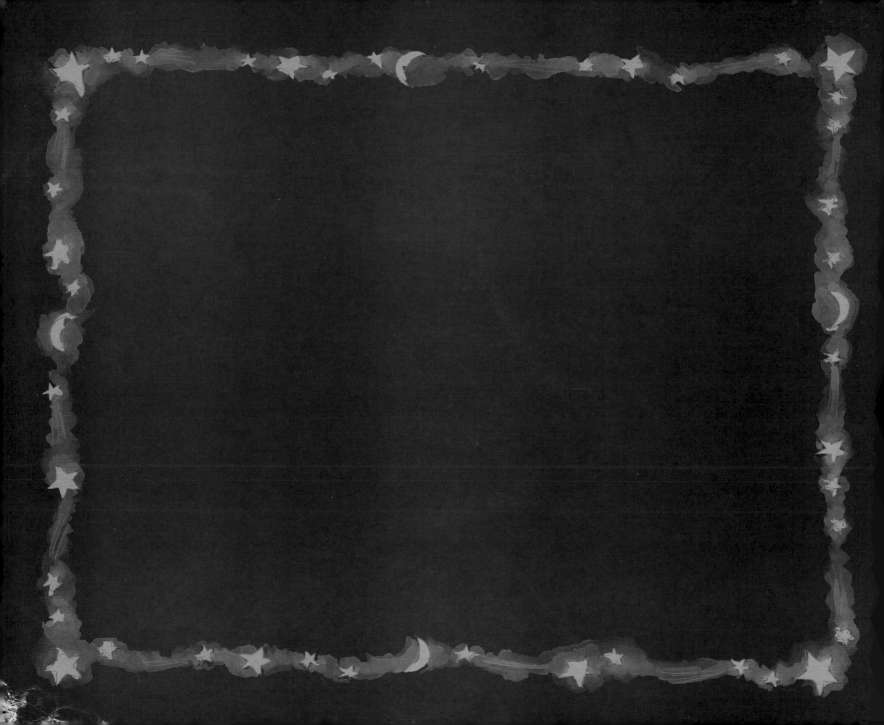